MW00629200

PRAY WHILE YOU'RE PREY

HOW GOD TURNED MY LONELINESS AND FRUSTRATION INTO CONTENTMENT AND COMMITMENT

PRAY WHILE YOU'RE PREY

HOW GOD TURNED MY LONELINESS AND FRUSTRATION INTO CONTENTMENT AND COMMITMENT

Toni L. Wortherly, Esq.

Copyright ©2004 Toni L. Wortherly, Esq. All rights reserved.
This book, or parts thereof, may not be reproduced in any form without permission from the publisher; exceptions are made for brief excerpts used in published reviews.

If you purchase this book without a cover, you should be aware that this book may have been stolen property and reported as "unsold and destroyed" to the publisher. In such case neither the author nor the publisher received any payment for this "stripped book"

Printed in the United States of America.

Toni L. Wortherly, Esq.
tonilashaunmusic.com

Cover Art by
Erica Wortherly

10 9 8 7 6 5 4 3

Scripture quotations are taken from the King James Version of the Bible.

This publication is designed to provide accurate and authoritative information with regard to the subject matter covered. It is sold with the understanding that the publisher is not engaged in rendering any professional advice. If legal advice or other expert assistance is required, the services of a competent professional person should be sought.
---From a Declaration of Principles jointly adopted by a Committee of the American Bar Association and a Committee of Publishers and Associations

DEDICATION

This book is dedicated to Jesus Christ and to single women and men throughout the world who are discovering His kindness, grace and mercy during their time of singleness.

ACKNOWLEDGEMENTS

To my Lord and Savior Jesus Christ

Thank You for saving my life and giving me a
purpose and the courage to pursue it.

To my Mom and Daddy

Thank you does not even begin to do justice to
what I owe you. You introduced me to God and
made sure that I knew the right way to live. You
introduced me to true love. You have supported
me through every up and down of my life,
emotionally, spiritually and financially. Rest
assured that my blessing will be your blessing.

To my big sister

Thank you for your inspiration and support.
Erica, thank you for using the incredible talents
that God gave you to make this book more
beautiful than I can ever imagine and for giving it
to me straight.

To my little brother

Thank you for giving me the support I needed to
step out on faith in forming my law firm. Having
my own business gave me the time to make this
book a reality and I could not have done it
without your sacrifice.

To my nephews and niece

Thank you for letting me sleep when I need to and not making me feel too guilty for being attached to my laptop. I will make it up to you.

To my best friend, Kimberly

Thank you for accepting my growth, and being there for me when I need you.

To my pastor and church

Thank you for your prayers and support for this endeavor.

Contents

HOW TO USE THIS BOOK EFFECTIVELY

This book is my story--my prayers, my struggles and my victory--but I have been told by those who have read early versions of it that they can identify with the experiences that God has allowed me to have. I have also been told that this book should be read section by section with time to reflect on what each part has to say. With this in mind, I have included some questions and instructions at the end of each section. Feel free to read this book at the pace you feel comfortable with, but I would like to suggest reading each section, looking up the Scriptures, and prayerfully considering it with the questions/instructions that accompany it.

It is my prayer that this book is a blessing to you.

Introduction

KNOW WHO'S IN CONTROL OF THE FOREST

"Whoso finds a wife finds a good thing and obtains favor in the Lord." I've read and heard it before, but one night it hit me like a ton of bricks. I was lying in bed contemplating my next move within my current relationship when I figured out what people had been telling me for so long. As many times as I'd heard that verse and had it interpreted for me, it wasn't until that night that it became clear. I am the hunted. I should be sought after. As a single Christian woman, I am PREY. It sounds really savage, but it's that basic.

I think a number of things contributed to my sudden clarity. That very day, I was the substitute teacher for a second grade class. During their writing workshop, my students wrote reports about animals. One of the report topics was the eating habits of the animal being researched. As I read through the reports, I saw how animals in the wild have special features and cunning ways for capturing prey. Although I don't want to be eaten, I too am prey to be hunted, chased, and pursued relentlessly, even after I am caught.

Later that night, I was told once again by

my brother-in-law that I am the hunted and he--whoever he is at the moment--should be hunting for me. It's as clear as day in the Bible. Of course, being an attorney, I always have an argument in my defense and in defense of my suitors. After all, it's not their fault that I have a controlling nature and an insatiable thirst for attention. I don't give them a chance to hunt me down. If I were a small animal, I'd be eaten every time I was hunted because I would be standing in the woods screaming, "Here I am! Come and get me! I'm ready to face my fate!" But the words of the proverb show that that is not the way that God intended it. Because it's the Bible, and the Bible only deals with the intended relationship of a man and a woman, the "whoso" in the verse refers to a man; the man that finds. You know, one day I asked my pastor if the use of the word "find" was literal. Again, my argumentative side likes to find loopholes in the system. My pas-tor explained to me that the word "find" could have a more figurative meaning. For instance, letting the man set the tone for the relationship or moving to the next level in the relationship. My main concern was, "What if I literally find him?" Like, I see him, and he doesn't see me, so I make myself known to him. At the time, I thought that was a legitimate point. But now I know that if God desires someone to be in my life, He will not keep that person from me. "He hath made everything beautiful in His time…" and there is "…a time to love.[2]"

So, what does it mean to find a wife? Find is defined as to become aware of, learn, notice, realize. So, the man who becomes aware of a precious woman of God, who learns her needs and desires, who notices her beauty inside and out and who realizes that he should love her even as Christ loves the Church, finds a good thing and obtains favor in the eyes of the Lord. The second "find" may have a slightly different meaning--to discover, locate, come across, unearth, stumble upon. A man discovers a precious gift, locates his other half, comes across a rare commodity, unearths an invaluable jewel, and stumbles upon something that is pleasing to God. The author of the proverb doesn't say whoso findeth a girlfriend, confidante or even a friend; he says whoso findeth a wife. And in order to be Godly wife material, a woman must know what God expects from her. She has to let him mold her into what He wants her to be. She has to trust and depend on God and only God. And, if she is like me, she has to learn to pray while she's prey.

1. Do you believe in Jesus Christ--that He died for your sins and is the living Son of God? If your answer is 'Yes,' move on to question 2. If your answer is no, turn to Appendix A to find out more about committing your life to Christ. Without a commitment to Christ, it is difficult for this book to be effective.

2. Do you believe that God is sovereign and that He has a plan for your life?

3. Name an instance in which God showed you that He is in control.

WHY AM I WRITING THIS?

From the time I knew what a relationship was, I have wanted to be in one. My parents are very much in love and have been for thirty years. They met in San Diego. They were both in the Navy. When my mom left home, she prayed for God to send her some-one who would take care of her. She asked that He send her a husband who would be good to her. She met my dad, they dated for six months, and then they were married. Forty years, three children, five grandchildren, and several military-motivated moves later, they are still like teenagers in puppy love. They not only love each other, but me, my siblings and all of our family and friends, no regardless of how we treat them. My parents are the type of couple that you look at and know that God placed them together because nothing could tear them apart. They are my inspiration. Their kind of love is so rare these days that it is clear that it is truly heavenly. They have had their issues. I don't think that you can be with one person for thirty years and not face adversity. But, they are constantly learning and growing in God and making things better every day. When I look at them, there is no sense of complacency. Every day is a new adventure and every day they seem to love each other even more.

Growing up around them, it was and still is hard not to want someone to love me the way that my dad loves my mom. It is also difficult for me not to have anyone to give my love to. Watching them, I have learned to love and nurture, which has built a yearning in me to love and be loved by someone. So, when I was younger, I sought love. I was an awkward kid. I was tall and skinny with big feet and no athletic talent. I knew what I wanted to be when I got older and I was interested in things like church and theater. Needless to say, I wasn't the most popular kid. Did I mention that in high school I wore glasses and braces? However, I still felt that I deserved to be loved and romanced. I went through three and a half years of high school with no one even interested in me. Finally, in my senior year I met a man who I thought could be the one. It didn't quite work out that way. I was seventeen and looking for a husband, and that's just not nor-mal these days. We dated for almost three years, but he wasn't ready for a commitment, so I cut him loose.

After having my braces off for a couple of years, getting contacts, and pledging one of the most elite sororities, I fell in love with me. I was conceited. I lived for me and only wanted to do what I wanted to do and not what I was supposed to do. During that time I "dated" (code for slept with guys), which only lowered my self-esteem. On the outside, I had things together, but on the inside, I longed to be in a loving marriage. Then, I was proposed to. In my mind, I thought that no one else would ever ask me. At the time, I prayed about it. I don't know if I listened for an answer, but I definitely prayed about it. And because I had prayed for a husband for so long, I thought that this was the answer to my prayer. I made so many compromises regarding my desires and prayers for marriage. Why would I think that God wouldn't give me just what I asked for? I don't know now, and I couldn't see the mistake I was making then. All I know is that my marriage resulted in heartache. We were divorced, and though few people can believe it, I still want to be married. I still want to love and be loved, but knowing what I know now, I will make sure that I move closer and closer to God to avoid past mistakes.

First, I want to be who God wants me to be, and I want to be able to accept the love that He sends. I want to have my own identity and be content with what I have. I want to use this time of being single wisely, so I have to pray for the prey--me. Of course, I don't just want anyone as a romantic suitor. I know the type of man that I desire, and I want to be with the type of man that God desires for me. I want to be accepting of men, but not too accepting, and I want my hunter to know how to pursue me, so I have to pray for my hunter. An animal in the forest being hunted would be praying not to get caught, but some human animals of the female species have an ultimate goal of getting caught. I just don't want to be overcome with loneliness before I'm hunted, and I want to be caught at the right time and under the right circumstances. I also don't want to let the blessing of a relationship make me lose focus or forget what God commands of me, so I have to pray during hunting season.

As I take this journey to discover what God wants me to see and do while I am prey, I want to write out prayers and scriptures that I use to get me through this experience. I want to remember my thoughts and meditations, so that my experience may help someone who hasn't yet realized that they are prey, or doesn't know which hunter to submit to, or what to do in the different stages of hunting season. I hope to learn and to teach others to pray while we're prey.

What has influenced your relationship expectations?

1. Now that you know why I wrote this book, take a few minutes to focus on your reasons for reading this book.

2. What is the biggest mistake you have ever made? Say it out loud. Forgive yourself out loud. Pray to God for His forgiveness and believe that He has forgiven you. Move on.

Part One

PRAYINGFORTHEHUNTED

My Prayer

Dear Lord, make me desirable prey. Lord, You have blessed me with salvation. You have given me a loving family and role models of good women in Your Word. You have given me unique beauty, style, grace and talents. You alone have made me and continue to mold me according to Your will. I want to be a virtuous woman. Lord, I want to use this time to grow closer to You. I am leaning and depending on You. I want to accept the call to holiness. Lord, please make me into the type of woman that a man of God will desire. Lord, I know that it is a man's job to find me, and I desire to be a woman worth finding. Help me to make room for a special someone in my life. Regardless of when You send my hunter, I need to know that I have to be dependent on You and that I cannot control every aspect of my life. Lord, help me to continue to find myself and have confidence in myself, not comparing myself to others. Help me to know that only You can complete me, change or enhance me. Help me to make the most of this time when I am by myself. I am Yours to give to him that You deem worthy when the time is right. I seek Your wisdom and guidance to evaluate every situation I encounter. In Your precious son Jesus' name I pray, *Amen*.

THE VIRTUOUS WOMAN[3]

I am praying to be a virtuous woman, like the one described in Proverbs. "Who can find a virtuous woman?[4]" That is a great question. Who can find a good, righteous, worthy, honorable, moral, upright, honest woman? I know that a man who is listening to God could find her. Who can be a good, righteous, worthy, honorable, moral, upright, honest woman? Any woman who is sincerely living her life for Christ will fit this description. And if she does fit this description, "her price is far beyond rubies." This powerful statement indicates to me that if I follow Christ's example and believe in God, I am an invaluable treasure. This should speak to a lot of women who are single and desire to be in a relationship. I have met many a woman who does not feel that she is worthy to truly have the best that God has to give her. We let our past and the things that we haven't forgiven ourselves for dictate our worth. As a divorcee, I have learned a wonderful lesson--when you confess your sins and truly repent, being honest with yourself and with God, He will forgive you for any and all mistakes, short of blaspheming against the Holy Spirit. Not only does He forgive you, but I know that He forgets. His Word says that He sets your sins as far as the East is from the West.[5] He wipes your slate clean. So, it's okay for you to have someone who will recognize that there is no more valuable jewel than you.

"The heart of her husband doth safely trust in her, so that he shall have no need of spoil.₆" This says a lot about what God will do for you in the relationship between you, His child, and the hunter He has sent you. In the past, I have been very insecure in relationships; always comparing myself to my partner's other options. I know that I am not alone in this insecurity and that men contribute to this feeling by commenting on other women. This verse speaks to me; telling me that I don't have to worry about any of that. If I am a virtuous woman, my mate has no need to look at any other woman. He has no need to stray because he trusts in all that God has made me. But it's not just the man that makes us nervous.

Now, I love women, but we are funny people. Let's face the facts. There are more women than there are men, which means a lot of cat fights, unless you are one of those women who would prefer to be single for the rest of her life. I know a lot of women look at me and other divorcees and think, "Now, they already had a chance to be married, so why should they get a second shot when there is a man shortage." Go ahead, admit it. I know that you or someone you know has had the thought. I know that we, as women, are often jealous of or threatened by women who are where we want to be. This is not a world phenomenon. It happens in church. I have seen many women give the evil eye to the woman who snared the last good-looking eligible bachelor in the church. And, women are not as innocent as we would like for everyone to think that we are. If we see the slightest opening in another woman's relationship, if we see that another woman is not "treating her man right," some of us will swoop in like birds of prey, ready to pick away at the carcass of a dying relationship. So, it's not hard to see why women are insecure in relationships. Yet, God says that the man he gives to his virtuous woman has no need for spoil, so that temptress can try as she may, but the hunter who caught you is not going anywhere.

"She…works willingly with her hands… she brings food from afar. She rises also while it is yet night and gives meat to her household, and a portion to her maidens…with the fruit of her hands she builds a vineyard. She girds her loins with strength and strengthens her arms."[7] The virtuous woman is not afraid of a little hard work. She can provide for herself, gives to her family and is generous to others. She's not afraid to get down and dirty and provide for herself and her loved ones. She is strong. As prey, we should strive to be a virtuous woman. We should be this diligent before ever meeting our hunter. Much has been said about the strong woman. Some find her to be intimidating, but this part of the story of the virtuous woman absolutely speaks to me, as I hope it speaks to you. We know that the virtuous woman gets a husband who knows he has a treasure, so why are we scared to be all that we can be? As an attorney, I cannot say how many times I have heard that it would be hard for me to get a man because I am considered scary. The fact that I was able to get up, get out and reach for my dreams and goals, while unattached, should motivate a man to want to be with me. The fact that I can provide for myself and am generous toward others should never be a turn-off. Any man who cannot see that your self-sufficiency and strength are not a threat is not your hunter. God created men and women in such a way that we need each other, but we can survive separately. I hate to see a woman waiting around for a man to take care of her. I often joke about marrying a rich man and I've been told that I need to marry a rich man because of my standard of living. But, rest assured that with God's help, I will work willingly with my hands to provide for me, my family and others, build my vineyard of goals and dreams, and continue to strengthen myself regardless of what my relationship status is at the time.

"She perceives her merchandise is good…"[8] Why would a hunter want to capture you if you don't even think you're worth the chase? Again, this goes back to self-worth. I have been on opposite ends of the spectrum of self-worth at different points in my life. I have had the occasion to think that I was the bottom of the barrel. I wasn't pretty enough; I was book-smart, but not street smart enough; I just wasn't…enough. Then, there were the times that I could give Narcissus a run for his money. The times when I was the greatest thing since sliced bread and everyone should stand and take notice or be left in my dust. Neither of those are the right place to be. When I read that the virtuous woman perceived her merchandise as good, I realize that I have to know and love all that is good about me in order to attract people who are good for me. I know you have probably heard it a million times before, but that is because it's true, and I'm about to say it again. If you don't love you, no one else can. I will take it a step further. If you don't love God's people, then you don't love God.⁹ If you profess to be a child of God, then you are one of His people that you have to love. If you don't love God, you will never be hunted by the right suitor. I have also learned when you are confident--not conceited-- but confident, you don't have to sell yourself. People are naturally curious about your "merchandise."

"She stretches out her hand to the poor; yea, she reaches forth her hands to the needy...Strength and honor are her clothing; and she shall rejoice in time to come. She opens her mouth with wisdom; and in her tongue is the law of kindness... [she] eats not the bread of idleness."¹⁰ To be a woman of virtue, life can't be all about you. Women are naturally nurturing, some of us more than others. We should use the time while we are single to do God's work and help His people like a virtuous woman. This part of the passage really gives me hope because it tells me that if I am considerate to those less fortunate, clothe myself in strength and honor, converse with God's wisdom and kindness, and combat laziness, I will have a time to rejoice and be jubilant. With or without a mate, I can live a full life that is pleasing to God, and I will be rewarded.

"Favor is deceitful, and beauty is vain, but a woman that fears the Lord, she shall be praised."[11] Finally, the passage provides motivation. The world we live in is caught up in celebrity and appearances, but those are deceitful and vain. I recently saw Halle Berry on the Oprah Winfrey show. She is a super-celebrity and considered to be the most beautiful woman in the world, yet neither of these attributes was able to help her sustain either of her two marriages. It was a resounding wake-up call. That which this world values is worthless. Celebrity and beauty can fade, but if you fear and revere the Lord God, no one can take that away from you. While I wait for my prince to arrive, I want to model myself after this virtuous woman. I want to be all that God wants me to be, not just for the sake of being in a good relationship with a man, but because when all is said and done, my relationship with God is the only one that matters.

1. Read Proverbs 31 in its entirety. List the characteristics of the virtuous woman. Which of these attributes do you possess?

2. Ask God to reveal the areas that you need to improve upon and bless you in your efforts.

3. What, besides your sin, are you beating yourself up about? List ten things that are wonderful about you. Focus on these things, and others will too.

A CALL TO HOLINESS

"In holiness and righteousness before him, all the days of our life...."[12] "[L]et us cleanse ourselves from unholiness from all filthiness of the flesh and spirit, perfecting holiness in the fear of God."[13] We were put on Earth to serve and praise God, but God knew that man should have a mate or companion, so he gave Eve to Adam.[14] However, the gift of Eve did not in any way diminish Adam's duty to God. Growing closer to God is our purpose; having a mate is a perk. Because of the fall of Adam and Eve, we are sinful creatures with the free will to do whatever we please. If we are among those chosen by God to have eternal life, our goal should be to please God and to be obedient. It is not easy, but it is also not impossible. It has taken me quite some time to learn that I will never have what I want unless and until I put God first. He must be first in everything. He must be our first love. In every decision we make and in every step of life that we take, we should consult God.

Some people think that the WWJD (What Would Jesus Do?) paraphernalia is just a bunch of trendy accessories, but it tells us how we should operate in our lives. Jesus Christ was proof that we could be human and not be filthy. Jesus Christ was proof that we could be blameless and clean. Some might argue that it is only because He was God and man at the same time that He was able to stand steadfast in the face of temptation. I submit that He was on Earth as a human to show us how our lives could be lived without filthiness. Each and every human who confesses the Lord Jesus Christ as his or her Savior has a never-ending obligation to seek holiness and righteousness in every deed. We cannot do that without God. Fear of God is the key to His secrets.[15] I do not speak of fear in the sense of being scared, but in the sense of reverence and respect. Reverence and respect for God and God's Word lead to strong confidence, refuge, contentment, and salvation from death.[16] God commands us to love Him above anyone or anything.[17]

God also wants us to love our neighbors as ourselves. It is a part of our call to holiness. "The Lord makes you increase and abide in love one toward another and toward all men, even as we do toward you to the end he may establish your hearts unblameable in holiness before God...."[18] "Beloved, let us love one another: for love is of God; and everyone that loves is born of God and knows God. He that loves not does not know God; for God is love."[19] Showing love to one another is a way to show our love for Christ. One of my biggest fears is that when this world is over, I will have been so consumed with my own "problems" that I will be held responsible for not loving God's people enough. It is so easy to fall into a trap of self-centeredness. We are supposed to love ourselves and take care of ourselves, but we are not supposed to be so self-involved that we forget about God's work and God's people. There are so many people in the world who have yet to discover the wonders of God. While we sit and complain about the things that we don't have, do we ever stop to think about how fortunate we are to have Christ? I have often heard it said and have at times said to myself that if God never blessed me with anything else, He has given me the gift of salvation, which is more than I could ever ask for. Too many of us take that for granted. We are not called to be holy to unlock a toy store full of blessings; we are called to holiness to share God's goodness with others and to spread the Gospel of Christ.

We show God our love for Him when we show others that we care. Being holy doesn't mean that we will always like other people. In truth, it is not the person that we don't like; it is his or her actions or attitudes that bother us. That is okay. Love doesn't mean accepting those things that are against God. It means having the patience to try to steer our brothers and sisters toward God. There are many different opportunities to strength-en our relationship with God in this way. I chose to teach a youth Bible study class. Others might go on missions to less fortunate countries or participate in other church outreach ministries. In any case, our love for God should never be kept a secret. That doesn't mean that we have to beat people with our Bibles or announce each and every good deed that we do. The worst thing that one can do when growing closer to Christ through love and work for others is to let our deeds for others overshadow our growth in Christ. When recognition becomes the reason for the deed, it is not done in love, and we move no closer to righteousness, holiness, or God. Remember the ultimate goal is to have the relationship with God that He intended us to have before the fall of man. It is not about us; it is about Him.

Being single gives us a unique opportunity to grow closer to God. "… [She] that is unmarried cares for the things that belong to the Lord, how [she] may please the Lord…There is a difference also between the wife and a virgin. The unmarried woman cares for the things of the Lord, that she may be holy in body and spirit…."[20] Before any hunt begins and before there is any capture, single women need to focus on their relationship with God. As single women, we can do that because we don't have the concerns that married women have. Some of us might have children who require a great deal of energy and focus, but the Word of God says that single women with no children are to care for the things of the Lord, and not the things of this world. So many times, and I'm guilty of it, we are caught up in finding a relationship or a career, and we forget that we should use this blessed time of singleness to increase our holiness. Who can blame us? From the time we are old enough to understand, we are inundated with different ideas of how life is supposed to be by familial and societal influences. We are told that we need to get through school, go to college, get a good career, get married, and have children. How many of us are ever told that we should grow closer to God? How many of us are ever told that we should take some time to get to know who we are through Christ? I promise you that you don't hear it on TV. So many of us think that our identity is wrapped up in our careers or who we marry or what kind of mother we become. The truth is that none of this matters if you don't have a good relationship with God.

I have learned much of this through hard lessons and am saddened to think about the time I wasted racing to a finish line that doesn't matter--a finish line that would give me status on Earth, but would do nothing for my soul. Through many trials and tribulations, brought on mostly by yours truly, I found out how easy it is to develop a relationship with Christ. I found out that it is much easier when you are single. Please don't ever quote me as saying that married people can't be close to God, because that's not what I'm saying. I am saying it's not as difficult to press towards holiness when you are the only person you are responsible for. Your decisions only affect you. Your moments of weakness are only experienced by you. There have been many nights when I woke up with a problem, or some sudden clarity, or just wanting to talk. It was a wonderful feeling to know that I had a friend who wouldn't curse me out for calling so late, who would listen to every word I had to say, and who would lead me down the best path that I could choose. That's the beauty of singleness. That's the blessing of singleness. I feel that once we stop fighting our singleness, we can grow much closer to God. I put my trust in Him for all that I do. I focus on pleasing Him and becoming who He wants me to be. I'm still growing, but now I know that I am growing in the right direction.

1. Take an inventory of your spiritual life? Do you pray regularly? Do you attend church regularly? Do you give of your time, talent and tithe regularly?

2. What area(s) of your spiritual life could use some help? What can you do to improve those areas?

3. What are some ministries in which you feel you would be effective?

Some of us have no problem with being single. (For those of us that do have a problem with it, I will address that issue later.) As a matter of fact, some of us rather enjoy our independence. Others of us are control freaks in every aspect of our lives, even though we know that God is the one who is truly in control. In either case, we cannot expect for our potential mate to give up his primal instinct to hunt. Women have to accept men as God intended them to be and make room for them in our lives if we don't intend to stay single. Now, I've heard it all, and I've said it all before. "I can do bad all by myself." Or, "I don't need a man in my life to make me happy." Or how about, "If you want something done right, you have to do it yourself." But ladies, if there's one thing I learned by trying to be my ex-husband's mother more than his friend, or by trying to put the men I'm interested in on a timetable or plan, it's that being too controlling or independent is the quickest way to emasculate a man. I'm not saying that you should learn to change your own oil or fix your carburetor. Let's not get ridiculous. I'm not saying that we have to be doormats or damsels in distress. What I am recommending is learning how to allow your hunter to find you.

Let him figure you out. If you must help the man out, take these pointers, which I have learned from my mistakes. Women are big on hints. Men don't like hints. If you are going to tell him something, just tell him flat out. Try not to add more detail than is necessary to get your point across. Let him try to help you solve a problem, even if you already think you know the answer. This is a serious problem for anyone who is naturally argumentative because we always want to be right. I can't believe I am about to say this, but it's okay to be wrong sometimes. You don't have to have all the answers. Even if your answer is right, his may be right too. As long as the problem is fixed, does it mat-ter who solved it? I promise you that it is easier for a woman to take one for the team when it comes to problem solving than it is for a man.

Now this is a real doozy, especially for the control freak. Let him determine where your relationship is going and then give him time to tell you in his own way. I used to operate on this crazy relationship timetable. Well, it didn't seem crazy until I really thought about it. Here goes: I meet him. In six months, we need to be dating exclusively. In a year, we need to be talking about marriage. After two years if we're not married, he's got to go. There are practical reasons for thinking this way. I only have so long to live, and I don't want to waste my life in dead-end relationships. I have learned a thing or two about how long it takes a man to realize what his feelings are, act on them and be able to express them. It's not that easy for some of us, and it's about ten times harder for most of them. No man wants to be forced into telling you that he loves you. No man wants to feel that he has no influence over the course of the relationship. If a man doesn't feel needed, he won't stay in the relationship.

Men are natural hunters. They like a challenge and they like to feel necessary. They don't like to be spoon-fed or ran over. I have witnessed this very thing with my older sister and her husband. She has been divorced and raising her three children on her own for about seven years. She has had help, but for the most part, she is a headstrong, independent woman. One day early in their relationship, her husband came over to her house and she was mowing the lawn. Now, my sister is petite, but she's a pretty strong, athletic woman. She's perfectly capable of pushing a lawn mower and a whole lot of other things that she's done pretty much on her own and in her own way for quite some time. But that day, he told her that he did not ever want to see her pushing the lawn mower again, and she willingly gave up the mower. It's not a matter of man's work or woman's work. It's a matter of letting the man do the things that make him feel like the man in a relationship.

Now, I promised I would get to the women who have a problem being by themselves. When I first thought about this sector of women, one in which I often find myself, I thought, "Well, clearly these women have made room in their lives for a man." Now that I look back on the times when I felt like I could not live without a man in my life, I know that there is such a thing as having too much room. It's a situation I've been in and seen over and over. A woman is in a relationship, breaks up with that man, and enters into another relationship before you can say, "Rebound!" It is a vicious cycle. When the verse says to make room for your man, I'm pretty sure that it doesn't mean to make a crater the size of the Grand Canyon. But for some of us, there is a huge void in our lives that we think should be filled by a man. Not so, my friends, not so. If you have a void in your life that seems unfillable, I submit to you that there is only one who can fill it, and He is Jesus Christ. When you feel needy, allow Him to be there for you because in my experience the only thing worse than a controlling or independent woman is a desperate, needy woman. Although men are hunters and love a challenge, there is such a thing as being too challenging. A man needs to feel necessary in the relationship, not necessary for you to continue breathing.

Be a gift in his life, not a burden. The time to work on that is before he finds you. If you are a control freak, try doing something that isn't in your day planner. Try letting someone else dictate your day. Try to compromise the next time you get into an argument. If you're throwing your hands up as Destiny's Child sings "Independent Women," try letting a friend pick up the tab every once in a while. Try hanging out with a group of people. If you are as needy as I find myself to be at times, try to figure out what causes you to feel empty. Ask God to help you fill the void in your life with His love and goodness. These actions will not only benefit you in all of your relationships, but also help when it is your time to be hunted.

1. Which characteristic do you identify with the most--independent, controlling, or needy?

2. What are the positive aspects of that characteristic? What are the negative aspects of that characteristic?

3. How has that characteristic affected your relationships?

THOU SHALT NOT COVET

Thou shalt not covet thy neighbor's house, thou shalt not covet thy neighbor's wife [or husband], nor his manservant, nor his maidservant, nor his ox, nor his ass, nor anything that is thy neighbor's."[22] So there I was minding my own business in the lounge at my law school, when a classmate and so-called friend of mine burst in the room in a huff. "What's the matter?" I asked. "I hate you," she replied. I thought for sure that she was kidding, but she wasn't. She began to berate me for having a husband, good grades and an active social life. She admitted, on more than one occasion, that she was jealous of me. If there was ever a clear depiction of exactly what the Bible tells us not to do in Exodus 20:17, this was it. Most of us aren't as bold as this sister because we envy in secret. Well, if you've been paying attention, you know that my marriage wasn't all that she thought it was. I was miserable, and the reason that I had good grades and an active social life was because I couldn't stand to go home at night. When I had to go home, studying was a perfect excuse to stay as far away from my ex-husband as possible. I don't think any one of us can look our-selves in the mirror and honestly say that we have never been jealous of the things that we think other people have. It's a natural, normal human response.

What needs to be explored is the root of jealousy. Why am I mad that my sister, my friend, my co-worker has a man, and I don't? Shouldn't I be glad that she's found love and hopeful that if it happened for her, it can happen for me? I know that sounds nice, but putting it into practice is the trick. I'll be the first to admit that it ain't easy because, as the Bible says, we will have battles between the Spirit and our flesh constantly.[23] The key is being content with what we have, and not worrying about what others have. Contentment does not mean never asking for any-thing else. Contentment means that if you don't get what you asked for, you're not going to curse God and stray from Him. God has a special blessing for each and every one of His children and He wants the best for us. The problem for a lot of us is that we don't know exactly what God has in store for us and when He will give it to us. If we knew what God was going to bless us with, then we wouldn't care about what someone else has, right? Wrong! We need to trust in God or trust in our own eyes; we can't have it both ways. The bottom line is that we shouldn't concern ourselves with whether what others have is what it seems to be from the outside looking in. We shouldn't even think about what God has given someone else other than to thank Him for blessing that person. And if the person is not of God, we really shouldn't care about her earthly possessions because our reward is in Heaven.[24]

Focus on being happy with how far God has brought you and pressing on toward your goals, without envy for others. Again, it's easier said than done, but with Christ all things are possible.₂₅ Having a mate is not the only area in your life in which God can bless you. I know from too much time spent at pity parties that if you focus on what you don't have, you will always come up short. If you have a problem focusing on the good things in your life, and spend your time focusing on the good things in others' lives, try this little exercise. Every ten minutes, write down something that God has done for you. If you're thinking that you won't be able to come up with something every ten minutes, then you don't truly realize the awesomeness of God. You have something to thank Him for every time you breathe. It goes a little something like this, God woke you up; He allows you to think, and He saved your soul from eternal damnation. That's thirty minutes worth of stuff right there. Really, it's a lifetime worth of blessings.

If you still have a problem with being grateful and content, rather than envious and miserable, play what I like to call the "What I DO Have" game. I know you've heard this one, "I once complained that I had no shoes until I met a man who had no feet." For me, it is usually, "My car is not a Mitsubishi Eclipse Spyder Convertible loaded with all the amenities, but a sturdy, dependable '95 Corolla that runs." Another one for me is, "I don't have a husband or children to love me unconditionally, but I get to make decisions without consulting anyone but God." Don't ever miss out on your blessings worrying about what someone else has. You have too much to be grateful for. If a blessing is meant for you, you will have it when God is ready to give it to you.

1. What is the difference between happiness and contentment?

2. Have you learned to be content in every situation?

3. Ask God to help you realize that His children have everything they need.

ENJOY YOUR "ME TIME"

As much as I've cursed this time of singleness and abstinence, I must say that it has been rewarding. I can admit that I haven't always been happy being single. If everyone was meant to be single, God would not have created Eve from Adam.26 There are days even as I write this when I have just screamed in anger, but those days, as my family will attest, do not occur nearly as often as they used to. The reason being that I have taken this time to find me. This is my "me time." For most of my life so far, I have lived to please other people, unbeknownst to them. That was my first mistake. I should be living to please God, and if I'm happy with me, then that's just an added bonus. When I was eight, I declared to the world that I would be an attorney. Low and behold, I am an attorney, but not because I want to be. I am an attorney because an eight-year-old with a big mouth wanted to be. I am truly grateful for my education. There are some things I would do differently, but I don't think that any of them would involve not getting my law degree. My real passion lies in entertainment. I have been acting and writing for the past eleven years, but being the eternal optimist that I am, I couldn't jump head first into either without a safety net. Until now, I just wasn't being fair to me because I didn't want to disappoint other people in my life.

At this point in my life, I am single in every sense of the word. I was blessed to escape from my marriage with no children. And in the past two years, I have been on two dates. In September of 2003 (which was after my graduation and before receiving my Bar results), I had to make some very tough decisions about my life. I had many talks with God. I am a pray-without-ceasing kind of girl.[27] I came to understand what that meant during this particular time in my life. I didn't know what I was supposed to do. I had a law degree, and I had to practice law because of the stipulations of my scholarship, yet I wanted to think about me for a change. That is the first time that I realized how truly blessed I am to be single. Because I am not married or even close to dating anyone, the decision was God's and mine. I started my own law firm. Having my own practice allows me to practice law in the fields that interest me and to pursue my other passions without any grief from a boss. The only mouth I had to worry about feeding was mine, and I am blessed to have parents that believe in me so much that they are willing to help with that part. They gave me a roof over my head, which was to be temporary, but has become indefinite. I tried to tell them that I couldn't leave and cleave when I got married if I wasn't with them in the first place, but that argument doesn't really work very well. My family gives me the moral and financial support that I need to make my current life work.

I also got a job substitute teaching so that I could ensure that I had income because I am a practical girl. Subbing was my main source of income at first, but now my clients pay my bills. On top of all of that, I have performed in three musical productions during the last six months. I don't live a life of extravagance. People look at me funny in the schools when I say I am an attorney. They don't understand the choices I've made, but I know that I made them prayerfully and with God. Furthermore, I know that I wouldn't have as many options if I wasn't single. I have witnessed this in the productions that I have been in. Women have had to leave rehearsal, not show up or bring their kids because the sitter bailed. Or women have had issues with their husbands about the amount of time that they spend at the theatre. I don't have to deal with any of that. And when I think about the way my life is right now, it is hard to complain about being single.

In addition to this time being a call for holiness, the single woman gets some "me time." If you are living your life the way I was, always trying to please others or keep up appearances, it can be very tiring. I have had to learn to take advantage of this time. I have had no choice. When I am not busy, I get bored very easily. When I get bored, I slip into the whining complaining version of myself. If I am going to be tired, it's going to be because I am working for God and myself, not wearing myself out for someone else. That may sound selfish, but if you're single, this is the time for a little selfishness. You always keep God first, and He will make sure that you are not crossing the line between being a little selfish and totally self-centered. So use your "me time." What is something that you haven't done because you've been so busy worrying about everyone else? Is there a passion you haven't pursued because you've focused so hard on being pursued? I had to answer those questions for myself. Though everything hasn't been easy, and some people think I'm nuts, things are working out just fine for me.

Even better, I know that when my hunter comes along, I will have my independence. Not the "I can do bad all by myself" independence that I spoke of before, but a lack of neediness. I won't need for my man to be in my face 24/7 because I have other things that take up my time. That doesn't mean that I won't make time, if he does, it means that I can lean and depend on God and the gifts He's given me. Having this type of independence also makes you more of a challenge, which, if we're being honest, is what most hunters are looking for.

1. What are your favorite activities? How much time do you spend doing them?

2. What are your goals for the next five years? Ten years? Twenty years? Are you working toward them?

3. Give yourself at least an hour each day to focus on self.

Part Two

PRAYING FOR THE HUNTER

My Prayer

Dear God, please send me a hunter. Send me someone in pursuit of all I have to give. Lord, let him be someone who knows You personally, not just on a superficial level, but on an intimate level. Let him be someone who will seek Your face during his quest for love. Let him be someone who knows that the only way to love me is to model himself after You. Lord, make sure that he is someone I'm attracted to, so that I can see him chasing after me. Lord, let him know and follow You as you teach him the way to my heart. *Amen.*

A HUNTING LICENSE

There are many different types of hunters. My inspiration was predators of the animal kingdom, but humans hunt too. When a human wants to hunt an animal, he (or she) has to get a license. Some people hunt for sport, some for trophies and some for food. Expert hunters study their prey, knowing how they sound, how they move, and what their vulnerabilities are. It would make life so much easier if the men hunting us fell into these categories. First, they would have to get a license that said they were ready, willing and able to hunt us. The license would have a mandatory waiting period, so that they could decide if they are really ready for the commitment that hunting requires. They could show us or our family and friends the license that listing their qualifications, like hunting experience (or past relationships if you will), weapons of choice (dating habits), and whether they hunt for sport (no commitment in sight), trophies (just to please others), or for food (looking for a wife). Having that information up front would really be helpful when we are approached by a man.

For example, about six months after my divorce, I was at a conference. It was really boring. On the last day, I was tempted to sleep in, but I didn't and for some reason, I decided to actually try to look decent. When I arrived in the conference room, I sat at the table with my friends and looked at the agenda for the day. The speakers took the platform and one of them took my breath away. There was just something about him. He was good-looking, but I could see even further than that. He had a confidence, a certain swagger that was extremely attractive. He spoke with such intelligence. I had to meet him. Most people who wanted to talk to him after the presentation were interested in his firm, but I was interested in him. I found out that he and I were from the same hometown, so I had something to talk to him about. When I did get the confidence to speak to him, it was just as I imagined it would be. He was just as sweet as he was smart, and to top it off, we had common friends back home. I glowed for the rest of the day.

A couple of days later, I e-mailed him, and we engaged in casual conversation. Then, we started to talk on the phone. We lived in different cities, so I didn't know how it would play out, but I had enjoyed his company by computer and phone. I knew that although I had initially approached him, I should let him set the pace of our relationship. About two months after we met, we went on a date. We had great fun that evening, and we laughed and joked and talked for hours into the morning. Our first kiss was like something out of the movies. I literally felt like I levitated off of the ground. It was the best kiss I had ever had (sorry to disappoint the other men I've dated). In the time that we kissed, my mind went from first date to sitting on the porch watching our grandchildren play. We continued to see each other for the next two weekends. Then, there was an abrupt halt. A few weeks before I was about to leave for a trip abroad, my dream guy told me that he just wanted to be friends. I meditated on that for a while.

One day, I saw a shirt that reminded me of him. He had played soccer, and there was a cool World Cup soccer shirt that I knew he would love. I had to give it one more shot and lay it on the line. I had to make him see how I felt about us. I told him my every thought from the time we met, but it was clear that we were not on the same page. He was hunting for sport. He had and still has no plans for a commitment. I was heartbroken, but I am glad that he eventually let me know that the relationship wouldn't blossom because there is nothing more miserable than being in a relationship with someone who doesn't want to be there with you. We continue to talk, and our relationship remains a friendship, with my not-so-secret fantasy that one day we'll be together. He is my Prince Charming. He came into my life when I was really at my lowest and helped me to see that I am worth more than I gave myself credit for. When I saw him from across the room that first day, I thought that he was way out of my league, but I can honestly say that I don't think he ever thought that. I can't say that back then if I had known that he never really wanted a relationship, I wouldn't have pursued him anyway, but I can definitely say it now. He was my ideal hunter in qualifications and weapons of choice, but not in the purpose for his hunt.

1. What are you looking for in your relationships (socializing, camaraderie, marriage)?

2. If there is a man in your life, ask God to reveal what he is looking for, because sometimes men say what they think you want to hear.

3. What has been the result in relationships in which you and your mate wanted different things?

THE IDEAL HUNTER

Every woman's ideal hunter is different. Some women are looking to date casually; some are looking for commitment. I don't know what category I would fall into at the present time. I would like to have someone to go out with on a regular basis. I don't think I am quite ready for a second marriage right now, but I also know that I don't want to be one of many women that a particular fellow is dating. The qualifications of the man of my dreams can be summed up with several "S" words. First, he must be SAVED, SANCTIFIED AND SEPARATED. This requires a true and intimate relationship with Christ. He needs to be pressing toward true discpleship, and it needs to be obvious. He can't follow the patterns of every man; he must follow the pattern of the Son of Man.

I desire someone who I find good-looking and SEXY. For me, that's someone who is taller than me with a medium build. I'm not partial to a particular race because I have had close friends of almost every race. My ideal suitor needs to be SMART. For most of my life, I have been recognized for my intelligence, and I need someone who is able to keep up with me. I need someone that I am able to talk to and debate with, but his intelligence doesn't have to come from a plethora of degrees. Another trait I desire is SUPPORTIVE. I have dreams and aspirations that revolve around my God-given talents. I only want to be around people who believe in the reality of my dreams. I don't want a "yes" man, but someone who is able to understand how much I don't want to lose the talents that I have.

For me, the ideal predator is someone who is SECURE. I need to be with someone who is confident enough in himself that he is not jealous, and he does not need me to validate him. There is nothing wrong with esteeming your man, but he shouldn't need it to survive.

I want the man who finds me to be STABLE in all senses of the word, emotionally, financially and mentally. I don't do well with other people's baggage. I have worked and prayed very hard to get rid of my own baggage. I need to be with someone who is in touch with his emotions, not stoic and unattached. He doesn't have to be a millionaire, but he has to be able to take care of himself and know how to deal with money. He has to know how to spend without getting into debt. I understand student loans, a mortgage, and a car note, but he has to have his priorities straight. I don't want to date someone who lives with his mother because he drives a Benz or a Beemer, and he can't afford his own place. Also, my captor needs to have a healthy mind. Having dealt with mentally unstable people, I prefer a sane gentleman, not one who is abusive, perverted, narcissistic or paranoid.

My hunter needs to be SENSITIVE--not a sissy, but sensitive. I am a sensitive person, so any suitor of mine has to understand how to not hurt my feelings. Finally, I need someone who has just the right level of SENSUALITY. Because of my upbringing, I am a very affectionate person, but affection doesn't always mean sex. I have learned that if two people have more sensuality in their relationship than they need at the time, it can cause confusing feelings to surface. So the man who hunts me needs to understand where to draw the line on intimacy.

Of course, none of this means anything if he is not ready for a relationship or not interested in me. For every woman who doesn't want to be single forever, there is one type of guy that she would recognize if he hunted her, but we cannot stop at the fact that he is or has all that we have hoped for. Some women (and men) may think that I ask for too much. I have no problem asking God for what I want because His word says that I can. If there is something he doesn't want to give me, He will say "no." My problem with asking for what I want is not being able to wait for him to give it to me.

There have been a few times, okay a lot of times, in my life when I have settled for less than what I asked God for. I have a big problem with letting God do His job, but I am working on that. I used to feel that I was too discriminatory and that maybe God was trying to teach me that I should give some guys the benefit of the doubt. I don't know where I got that warped thinking when the Bible clearly says that if I believe that I will receive whatever I desire when I pray, I will have them.[28] It doesn't say that it might be done or that it will be done with a few caveats. It says it shall be done. It's right there in the Bible. But there are times when I, and maybe some of you, over think God's Word. It's not just that it will only happen if it's charitable or reasonable. I know that there have been times in my life when I have begged for things, and God has let them happen even though they were ludicrous. He will let us learn our lesson about asking for ridiculousness if we ask Him enough.

Remember the Israelites and their request for a king? They didn't need a king; they had the King of Kings looking out for them, but they couldn't see Him so they begged for a ruler. He gave them Saul. Saul was good-looking and one heck of a warrior, but Saul wasn't all that he was cracked up to be. Saul got too full of himself and forgot that it was God who was still in control. Saul didn't listen to God's instructions, so God replaced him.[29] It goes to show us that God will give us exactly what we ask for just so He can show us that we are asking for the wrong things.

Now, if He'll give us the crazy things that we beg for, why wouldn't He give us those things which are perfectly reason-able? Further, a woman of God cannot just accept that a man has the outer appearance of being what she asked for. She has to give the man a chance to show and prove it. We have to let him do what God instructed him to do. We have to let him find us and pray that he knows God's instructions on being a good person and a good husband (if that's what you're waiting for). Every man who hunts us will not be husband material, so we have to stay prayed up and be on the lookout.

1. Imagine that you are preparing for a date and he arrives early. Would God, as your father, let your dates in? Do the men you date meet his standards?

2. Describe your ideal man in every detail you can think of? Review your list to make sure that saved, sanctified and separated are on that list.

3. Pray that God will send the hunter you want when the time is right. Believe that God will answer every aspect of your prayer.

A PIECE OF COAL VS. A SLUG

This might sound weird, but I promise that in the end it will all make sense. Because I know what qualities I desire my hunter to have, on many occasions in my life, I have been called out for being a snob. I used to feel guilty about it. People would often tell me that if I wasn't careful, I would miss out on an opportunity for someone I might really like. I have also been told on several occasions that I have narrowed my own field by my personal requirements. For example, I need to date someone with at least a bachelor's degree or the equivalent in life experience. I'm not being stuck-up, I would like to have something to talk with the man about and school has taken up the greater part of my life at this point. Also, I do not date men with children. I have nothing against responsible, single fathers, but this is a major point of contention. I know that a child doesn't fit into my lifestyle right now because I know that I am a glutton for attention and that I want to be my hunter's first priority after God. If I am dating someone who has a child, I want the child to be the most important person in his life. Those two ideals just cannot co-exist. The point is that I have a pretty good idea of the things that I will and will not accept in a mate.

One night I had a conversation with my father, mother, and a close friend about this very subject. My dad felt that we young women were a little too hard on men. We expected too much too soon. He told us that when he met my mom, he was a skinny, nerdy country kid from South Carolina. He hadn't finished college or grown into the handsome man he is today. He claims that due to our standards, we would have looked past him because he was a diamond in the rough, maybe even a piece of coal.

You see, diamonds and coal aren't very different. First of all, coal is not just carbon. It is a mixture of molecules from ancient plants, fungi, and bacteria. Heat and pressure change coal's chemical composition over time so that it becomes nearly pure carbon in the form of graphite. The difference between graphite and diamonds is in the arrangement of the carbon atoms in the material. If the sheets of graphite are pressed close enough, the carbon atoms will be make the bonds of a diamond. Therefore, a piece of coal is just a diamond in the rough. Once all of the ancient plants, fungi and bacteria are removed, all that has to be changed is its arrangement for it to become a diamond. Coal is that guy who just needs to go through his natural maturation process, and then God can re-arrange his structure, so that he is a diamond.

I told my father that I had given a diamond in the rough a chance. In 1999, when my ex-husband approached me, I had an open mind. When he told me that he was two years younger than me, it didn't bother me because every man that I'd met between the ages of 18 and 24 were on the same level of maturity. They still loved video games and hanging out with the boys, so I thought, "age ain't nothing but a number." Then, he told me about some problems that he had had in the past…legal problems. At the time, I had a "save the world from injustice" attitude. I believed then and still do that he was a victim of a flawed system of justice, so I let that slide.

He then told me that he lived with his mother, but it was only because of his recent legal issues, and he would move out as soon as he had the money. And, while he was there, he was helping his mom out and paying some bills. Other than that, he seemed generous and sweet. He proclaimed his salvation, and he attended church as much, if not more, than I did at the time. I thought that whatever issues he had, I was in no position to judge. After all, everyone has made mistakes, and everyone has things that they are not proud of; most of us just never get caught. I thought of him as a diamond in the rough. He had a lot of ambition, or so I thought, and with God's and my guidance, that piece of coal could be squeezed until it became a shiny diamond. I encountered several problems with my plan.

First, I thought that I could change a person. No human being has the ability to change another human being. If the hunter doesn't come into your life in the way that will best benefit you, chances are he will not change. Next, I was too open-minded. I believed (blindly) everything that came out of my ex-husband's mouth. Unfortunately for me, none of his lies caught up to him until after we were married.

That's not to say that we didn't have issues during our courtship and engagement, but because I believed whole-heartedly in his relationship with God and because I wanted too badly to be a married woman, I figured we could fix the little things that came up. Funny how they seemed little then; to most people they were huge. For three years, I tried to make my little piece of coal into a diamond, but alas, I failed.

My father's theory is that he wasn't a piece of coal at all, he was a slug. I don't know what slugs look like anywhere else, but here they actually are a dark black coal-like color. They move so slowly that you can't tell if they are an inanimate object or not. I imagine that if you pick one up it is pretty sticky, but it appears to be smooth just like the coal. In any case, no matter what conditions you put it under, or how you arrange it, it would never become a diamond. Not even a rough diamond. So how can you tell the difference between a piece of coal that has the potential to become a diamond and a slug that only appears to have that potential? My honest answer is that God is the only way to tell. We can't see with our naked eyes what God has in store for some-one's life. Only He knows who is really going to be somebody and who is going to move so slowly that he is virtually stagnant. God knows which men He will re-arrange into diamonds and which ones don't even know Him and, therefore, never had the potential to become diamonds. I have learned that the more my relationship with Christ grows the easier it will be for me to tell the difference.

Further, I feel that if God has planned for someone to be in my life, I will truly (not just because I am convincing myself to see something, so I don't look like a fool) see that person as a finished product. So, I no longer feel guilty about waiting for a hunter who has the qualities that I need and want. By faith, I believe that the hunter with my desires will be made known to me, and you should believe that as well. Delight yourself in the Lord; and he will give you the desires of your heart. Commit your ways to the Lord; trust also in him; and he shall bring it to pass.30

1. Do you attract more coal (diamonds in the rough) or slugs? Why do you think that is?

2. Ask God for the gift of discernment, so that you can tell the difference.

ANIMAL INSTINCTS

W hat kind of hunter are you dealing with? I have spoken about human hunters of animals, but let's get to the real inspiration behind my whole line of thinking…animals. Different animals have different ways of hunting their prey. Here are some examples of how different animals hunt and how their methods of hunting can be exhibited by the human male. Now, some might ask after reading this section why six animals are listed, but only two have truly desirable hunting (dating) methods? My answer is for you to think about all of the men who you have ever dated to see if one-third of your potential mates were worth your time. For me, I wish I could say one out of ten, but I'm still 0-for-who knows how many, so in my humble opinion, two out of six ain't bad.

The coyote is an opportunist, eating small animals and fruit. It usually hunts by itself, but may combine efforts with one or two others to tire prey. Sometimes while another animal digs for rodents at one end of a burrow, a coyote waits to pounce on any that emerge from an escape hole at the other end.

The coyote is the man who doesn't want to do any of the work. He finds you after you have been worn down by other men in your life. He finds you when you're ducking and dodging the men of your past and then he surprises you. This is that guy that approaches you before you even break up with your current man. He sees you on that day when you're fighting mad with your mate, and then he swoops in with his charm and grace. Such charm and grace are amplified by the fact that you're upset with someone else. He seems innocent enough, just sitting there waiting, but what he's really doing is waiting to pounce when your defenses are down.

The wolf pack works together on a hunt, either chasing down its victim or forcing it back to waiting pack members. It hunts at night and can go for two weeks or more without food. It gorges itself when food is plentiful. Wolves do not attempt long chases. If they cannot capture running prey after a while, they abandon the attempt. Wolves try to surprise prey and cut off its retreat, or ambush it. When an animal runs away, the wolf's instinct is to dash after it, but it is soon apt to give up such a chase unless the pursued creature stops and starts intermittently. Wolves test prey, looking for signals of the possibility of its defeat, and the pack often continues to pursue it.

I like to think of the wolf as that guy who is always around his friends. He sends one friend over to talk him up. Or maybe he sends a friend over to fish out your weaknesses. Being in the presence of so many people can sometimes be so intimidating that a woman will abandon her natural instincts for fear of embarrassing herself or her man. This man will run after you if you try to run away. He'll send you flowers or candy or try to make up. But he is not likely to do this more than once. He doesn't like a long chase, and since he can go for weeks without you, why would he chase you down. He will test you to see what you will put up with, and the moment he sees a weakness, he will strike. If he knows that chocolate-covered popcorn is all it takes, then that's what he'll do. And when he is no longer interested, he is willing to tell his friends all they need to know about you, so that one of them can hunt you next.

The grizzly bear is omnivorous. It feeds on a wide variety of plant material, as well as fish, insects, and large and small mammals. It is adept at catching fish, snapping them up quickly or holding them down until reaching in to get it. It feasts on the remains of larger mammals, such as elk, moose, mountain goats, sheep, or livestock. More often, it establishes dominance through size and threats. The grizzly bear isn't all that choosy. If it can hunt you, it will. It can snatch you up quickly or wear you down until you're easy prey. This man is another one who will feast on your remains. He would rather hunt you when your standards aren't that high. Or he will use intimidation and dominance to get you to give him a chance.

Eagles are fish eaters. When they pursue their prey, they snatch the fish from the surface with their talons. They have excellent vision and obtain much of their food by stealing it from the smaller "fish hawk." The eagle is the man who is superficial, not willing to dig deeper to see what is beneath your surface. He may feel that he doesn't have to look deeper. His excellent vision helps him discern who is ready to be caught. And if this man doesn't feel like doing the work himself, he can always steal you from someone who's weaker. He can watch and wait while that man who is less attractive, less financially stable, or just less than he is hunts you down. Then, he will swoop in and steal you without having to do anything that he is capable of.

The jaguar hunts mostly on ground, but climbs well and sometimes ambushes prey by leaping from tree limbs or ledges. Unlike most cats, the jaguar is very fond of water and hunts in streams for fish and other aquatic life. It has incredibly powerful jaws and can haul a full-grown cow for a mile. The jaguar is that guy that just surprises you. He's not like the other guys. He doesn't hang out in the same places that they hang out, and he doesn't look for the kind of girls that they look for. He is willing to stray from his routine, maybe even go out of his way for the sake of the hunt. He is not just a fun guy. He is a strong guy. He is in it for the long haul. His charm can draw even the most unwilling prey because that's just how cool he is.

The mountain lion hunts day or night, although by day only in undisturbed areas to avoid humans, choosing to hunt at night in populated areas. It is a good climber and excellent jumper. Sometimes it waits for passing game, but more often it travels widely after prey. It can outrun a deer, but only for short distances. After locating large prey, it usually slinks forward slowly and silently with its belly low to the ground and legs tensed to leap. It tries to stalk before running from its hiding place and leaping onto its victim's back, keeping its hind legs on the ground for support, control, and stability. The mountain lion is that man who appears from nowhere. He likes quiet places by day, but he likes to be where the crowd is at night, so he's not easily detected.

He is the one who sees you from afar and takes notes. He knows what makes you laugh, what song you always dance to; he takes his time to know you. Then, he slinks closer and closer. Most likely, you don't even know that he's there observing you. His pursuit of you is very surprising. You think that it is spontaneous, but it is actually very calculated. While it might sound like he's stalking you, he really just doesn't want to waste his time or yours. He will be one step ahead of you for a while, but soon you will catch on to him. Even when he catches you, he's got your back, always steady and supportive.

Obviously, there are many other types of hunters and some men are combinations of different hunters. A woman has to be careful of whose hunt she succumbs to. The only way to do so is to seek God's guidance.

1. Review the list of predators. Do any of them seem familiar? Which ones?

2. Which predators do you attract the most? The ones that work for you? The ones that prey on your weaknesses? The ones that give up on a challenge?

3. What hunting methods do you respond to the most? Is that good or bad?

Part Three

PRAYING DURING HUNTING SEASON

My Prayer

My Lord, you have to know that I love you, but
this is hard. God they are building all kinds of
new restaurants all around me, but I have no one
to go with. Each weekend blurs into the week, as
I spend it working and trying to pass the time
because I don't have someone to spend it with.
I'm lonely Lord. I know that you are here with
me all of the time, but I can't hug you or hold
you, and if I laugh or talk with you in public,
people will think I'm crazy. I love my family and
my friends, but they can't fill the hole that is in
my life. Lord, you've blessed me with so much,
and I know I didn't deserve any of it. Lord, you
know I want to get married, but I can't do that
unless I date, and I don't want to make the
mistakes that I've made in the past. Lord, please
suppress this loneliness, help me find a focus,
and when the right hunter comes along, let me be
ready to let him hunt me. Let me be willing to
accept his efforts and not try to rush things along
in my usual way. Lord, let me not be led into
temptation and deliver me from evil. I know that
You are all I need to survive this time in my life.
Amen.

OPEN SEASON

"Let him kiss me with the kisses of his mouth: for your kiss is better than wine...tell me, thou whom my soul loves, where you feed, where you make your flock to rest at noon...your cheeks are comely with rows of jewels, your neck with chains of gold...behold you are fair my beloved, yea, pleasant."[31] Some of the most beautiful love poetry and stories can be found right in the Bible. If you're looking for a good romance novel, thumb through Song of Solomon some-time. The lovers in those passages are so passionate about each other. I mean I wouldn't mind having a man after me who thought that "many waters cannot quench love, neither can the floods drown it."[32]

Most women dream of having a relationship full of romance and mutual adoration. If you grew up watching soap operas like I did, you have an unrealistic expectation of what romance should be like. In all of my soap operas, the two lovers are either star-crossed or bitter rivals. Then, some adversity or tragedy brings them closer together. Once they start dating, they always go to the nicest restaurants and on vacations to the most exotic places. Even their arguments are passionate. Then, they get married. Some stay happy, while others divorce and start the process all over again. It all seems so ideal, but life isn't like that. Thank God life isn't a daytime drama because you can end up dating your brother on one of those shows. In order for your love story to be great, there are certain practical issues that you have to deal with before and during hunting season. Because we don't usually get to see these issues resolved on TV or in movies, I will deal with them as I see them.

I don't know about anyone else, but I can't think of a time in my life when I was constantly being pursued, so before I ever deal with a chase I have to battle with loneliness. Then, there are the pressures of being in a dating relationship. How do you stay focused on your relationship with God when you're in a relationship? How is it possible to stay celibate? When are we going to get married? Because every single man and woman is different, different issues come up in a couple's dating life. I can only speak to those that I have been personally affected by.

1.   What is the biggest challenge posed by being single (i.e. loneliness, temptation)?

2.   If you are not challenged by your singleness, say a prayer of thanksgiving.

COMBATING LONELINESS

I say combating loneliness because for me, it's all out warfare. One of the greatest foes of my short life has been loneliness. I can only imagine that it has been that way because my relationship with God is not what it should be. During my first year of college, while I was still dating my first boyfriend, I was extremely homesick. I was in Virginia, and my family was in Florida. The one uncle who I could visit was moving to North Carolina. My boyfriend transferred back home to a school in Florida. My roommate and I had a love/hate relationship. I can't even say that we were friends. I had only just begun to make one friend in my dorm, but, all in all, I felt alone in the world. Every person who had been my comfort and my strength was nowhere to be found. My homesickness took on physical symptoms, and I became more and more ill during my second semester of college.

One night, when I was sick at home and my roommate was out, I experienced a heart-wrenching loneliness. My boyfriend was nowhere to be found. My family didn't answer the phone when I called. I couldn't understand why God wouldn't let me have anyone in my life. I thought long and hard about whether anyone really cared about me. I thought I might put it to the test. So I stared down a bottle of allergy pills. One made me sleep for 12 hours. So I figured three would make me go down for about a day and a half. I didn't want my life to end. I just wanted the loneliness to end, and if I couldn't be revived for 36 hours, someone would have to take care of me. I know now that those thoughts were completely irrational and totally lacked faith, but at 18, it seemed reasonable. I held the pills and thought to myself about the possibility of them killing me, but, for a chance at not being lonely anymore, I was willing to take the risk. I poured a glass of water and sat at my desk. I actually even prayed.

As I sat there, I began to hear a gospel song that my mom had played when I was younger. It talked about Jesus' friendship--how Jesus sticks closer than any brother. I knew at that moment that I was never alone because God promised that he would never leave me, nor forsake me. I cried and cried and threw the pills in the garbage.

I am not saying that I am never lonely, but I know that the world could be devoid of all human life, except me and God would still be there with me. Even when He was going to die for our sins, He promised that we would never be alone. "But the Comforter, which is the Holy Ghost, whom the Father will send in my name, He shall teach you all things and bring all things to your remembrance, whatsoever I have said unto you."[33] That night, the Holy Spirit reminded me that Jesus was the only friend I ever need, the only family I ever need, and He is my Savior. For the Lord says, "Fear not, I am with you: be not dismayed; for I am thy God: I will strengthen you; yea, I will help you; yea, I will uphold you with the right hand of my righteousness."[34] I honestly believe that loneliness is one of the devil's favorite weapons. In my life, there hasn't been a more powerful weapon.

Loneliness has caused me to go through every emotion from extreme sadness to utter rage. I got married because I was lonely, only to discover that I was even more lonely in that relationship. Loneliness has caused me to go out to parties and drink too much to try to numb the pain. It has caused me to throw myself at men who weren't even deserving of me. Even to this day, there are times when I cry myself to sleep because I am lonely.

It seems ridiculous to think that I have a growing relationship with Christ, a loving family who would do anything for me, and awesome friends who are there just at the right time, and I am still lonely. It's because I attribute my loneliness to not having a man in my life. There is nothing wrong with wanting to be hugged and held by a man. We are humans, and many of us crave affection and attention. If I'm not a point in my life where God wants me in a relationship now, yet I still focus on not having a relationship, I will always feel lonely. The man doesn't make my loneliness go away; the mindset makes my loneliness go away.

If I accept each and every point in my life as the place where God wants me to be, so that He can help me grow and prepare for the next place He wants me to be, then how can I be overcome by loneliness? There are times when we need to be all by ourselves, so that God can

get through to us. I am still learning to accept
that.

1. What is the difference between being
    alone and being lonely?

2. If you are a child of God, are you ever
    alone?

3. Anytime you feel lonely or alone, ask
    God to comfort you.

FOCUS FOCUS FOCUS

My sister is constantly telling me that my focus is all wrong when I'm being hunted and when I'm not. And though I hesitate to admit it, she is absolutely right. I am still learning that Jesus is all, day by day. And when my hunter finds me, I have to be careful that I don't focus on the hunter and the hunt. As long as I continue to grow closer to God and keep my focus on God and all that He is to me, everything that is supposed to fall in place will fall in place. It sounds simple enough, but it's not. It's really easy to become twitterpated (for those of you who haven't seen "Bambi," substitute "caught up" for "twitterpated") and daydream about the dream man who has not only found you, but is now pursuing you. We are human and most of us have a desire to have a companion. However, the hunt should never interfere with our relationship with God.

In my experience, men will say ANYTHING to get what they want. You meet him, and you divulge that you are a Christian. He says that he is a Christian, too. You go out to eat, and he says grace over the food without hesitation. You spend the night at his house and catch a glimpse of him on his knees praying before bedtime (of course this is only because your car broke down or there is a terrible rain storm and he sleeps on the couch - wink wink). Girl, he even started going to your church. Oh, now we've found a winner. Well, don't start sounding the bells and whistles yet. Any person can endure a couple of weeks, months, or maybe even years of pretending to be focused on God, as long as they are getting what they want. I wouldn't say it if I hadn't gone through it.

It is easy to think that your new man is focusing on God just as much as you are. But what do his actions indicate? If he is pressuring you for sex, somehow I don't think that his focus is that strong. I know that he's a man, and men have needs whether they are Christians or not, but don't buy into that. If he insists that it would be better for you to start "meditating" at home over Sunday brunch instead of going to church because you want to spend more time with your hunter "growing closer spiritually," you need to raise an eyebrow. Anyone who makes you take your focus off of God is not good for you. If he is really focused on God, he will have a purpose of pleasing God and making sure that your relationship is pleasing to God.

Equally as important, don't voluntarily lose focus. Don't plan your week around your relationship. Plan your relationship around your week. There are things that you are to do for God every day, and a relationship, especially one that God gave us, should never get in the way. Talk to God more than you talk to your man. Don't skip choir rehearsal because your man wants to go on a picnic. Don't miss Sunday School because you and your new beau stayed out really late on Saturday night. If the only time he has available to go out with you is on

Wednesday during Bible Study, invite him to Bible Study. (P.S. If this hunter is truly a man of God, he won't allow this to happen anyway.) God doesn't allow us to be in relationships so that we can forget all about him. He is a jealous God.35 Our focus should be on pleasing Him at all times whether in a relationship or not.

If you need an illustration of how important focus is, think about when Peter wanted to walk on water. As long as he focused on Jesus, he could walk on water, but when he focused on the water, he sank.36 As long as you focus on Christ, you'll sail easily through your relationships, but when you focus on the relationship, it will sink. God doesn't want us to be alone if we desire not to be. But any time that you put anyone or anything before God, it is a sin and displeasing to God. God will not bless anything that is displeasing to him.

1. What aspects of your relationships cause you to lose focus on God?

2. If you are in a relationship, make a pact with your hunter that you will keep God first in your relationship.

3. If you are not in a relationship, focus on weak areas in your relationship with Christ while you wait for him to send your hunter.

BEING CHASTE WHILE BEING CHASTE

It's amazing how the children that I teach inspire me. I have unwillingly overheard a conversation between two young girls, who can't be more than 17, about being scared of pregnancy. I think back to my senior year of high school. I was what some might consider a prude. I just knew that I'd wait until marriage and I didn't want to be a part of any conversation that involved giving up my precious gift. Yet, here I sit near girls ten years my junior talking nonchalantly about sex, its issues and effects. For a single woman sex is an issue.

As a woman, I have realized that the consequences of a nonchalant attitude toward sex are extremely detrimental. One of the biggest differences between men and women is our attitudes about sex. Of course, I speak in generalities. There are always exceptions, but to my knowledge, for women, sex is an act of emotion. Sometimes it may seem as if it is just physical, but no matter how hard you try to escape it, women get emotional when it comes to sexual intercourse.

WARNING: the following may seem graphic, but, in my humble opinion, it is just real. How can you not have emotions about a person with whom you enter into an act that involves that person becoming one with your body? Every aspect of the act is so intimate that it is hard to fathom that some people engage in sexual acts with callousness.

I'll admit that I tried it. I was fed up with guys treating me any kind of way. And at the time, I thought that guys were only good for one thing anyway, so I might as well use them for that one purpose. It didn't quite work out that way. No matter how hard I tried to convince myself that my relationships were just physical, a part of me always longed to have that person in my life for more than just that night. In my mind, (pardon my crassness) if I could put it down good enough, they wouldn't go anywhere. Why couldn't I, a woman, do what so many men do daily? Well, for starters, I have always known the right thing to do. From the time I was old enough to talk about sex, I knew that it should be reserved for marriage--for that one special per-son--because the amount of emotion involved in that act of intimacy can't be shared with a multitude of people. Not to menntion that the Word of God is very clear about fornication, which is defined as sexual relations outside the marriage.

In Acts 15:20, James declared that the apostles should write to the Gentiles and tell them to abstain from fornication. "For this is the will of God, even your sanctification, that you abstain from fornication."[37] Even now, I shudder to think that I risked my sanctification and my relationship with God for 15 minutes of so-called pleasure. I'm not saying that sex is bad.

During the better times of my marriage, I enjoyed it but that's just it--I was married. Sex no longer carried the guilt that it did when I was outside the will of God. It became something beautiful rather than tawdry. After my divorce, I looked for the loophole. I rationalized that because I had already been married, I was not having sex before marriage. Trust me, I knew the theory was flawed, but I was looking for an excuse. Sex is a powerful thing and I don't think that people always realize that. That's why it is reserved for a married couple. Single women not only have emotional consequences of attachment and distorted feelings of love, but also the possibilities of pregnancy and disease--things that stay with you for the rest of your life. Although God forgives us for sexual transgressions made in the name of "love" or lust, the consequences don't necessarily go away.

It's hard enough to be pure and holy when you are alone, but once you meet your hunter, it's even harder. Here's the man who has everything that you've prayed for, and now he's getting to know you and catering to your needs. Chastity is still required.

I can only speak from my experience. After making it through high school with my virginity intact, I met a man who I thought was perfect at the time, and we figured that because we planned on getting married, it was okay to "make love." Ah, making love sounds so much more innocent than sex or fornication, which is what it actually is. Well, as you now know, that relationship didn't work out, so my goal of being pure for my husband was no longer an option. I tell you this so you can understand the reason for waiting until you are married. A hunt doesn't always result in a capture. Pregnancy, disease, your emotions and your sanctification are huge risks for the sake of physical "pleasure."

I thought returning to abstinence would be the hardest thing I would ever have to do. It is definitely a one-day-at-a-time process. It is human nature to find pleasure in sex, but the spiritual nature should win the battle. For me, it was a lesson in saying no, and not getting into situations where it is difficult or next to impossible to say no. It's never too late to say no, but if you're buck naked in a bed, it makes it a teensy bit more difficult. I had to get over my fear of disappointing the man. Who cares if I disappoint him? He is not the one who will give me eternal life. What about disappointing God? I am not living for that man. I am living for Christ, and if he is living for Christ, then he should not pressure me for sex. If he's not living for Christ, then I have no business with him.

I know a couple who has known each other for three years and dated for two and a half. They are engaged to be married. I am around this couple a lot and can count on one hand the number of times I have seen them kiss. They practice celibacy, and their relationship inspired me to give up the physical. They showed me that it could be done. These are two very attractive people who, for some reason that can only be God, can keep their relationship pure.

I am an affectionate person, so I am likely to be in a relationship that involves more kissing, but I know my limits. Of course, since I haven't seriously dated anyone while I have been on my celibacy journey, I haven't truly been tested. But I have so much invested in my renewed purity and I feel so much closer to God, that I am confident of my ability to keep fornication and sexual impurity out of my life. I am very outspoken about my celibate lifestyle now, which some of my friends don't appreciate, but I know the difference that it has made in me. If you want an instant self-image booster, stop giving away pieces of yourself to potential mates.

1. Right now, make a commitment to Christ that your will keep you body pure until you are married.

2. If you are extremely sensitive to sexual innuendo, make a list of movies, television shows, magazines, etc. that you need to avoid.

3. Find a hobby. Last summer I started baking and crocheting; both are very therapeutic during times of temptation.

THE LUST FOR MARRIAGE

From birth, a girl is surrounded by images of marriage. All of the fairytale princesses get married and live happily ever after. Some grow up like me with deliriously happy married parents. Some dream of the deliriously happily married life that their parents never had. On television, in magazines, in movies, it seems that women are not happy unless they are married or getting married or being pursued by a man. As a young girl grows, she is told what kind of girl a man likes. Then, when she is of marrying age, and still not married, she is constantly bombarded with the questions of when and with whom she will settle down. Of course, not all women deal with this, but for me, singleness never seemed like an option.

When people think of lust, they think of some uncontrollable sexual desire--a desire for physical love. But my lust had very little to do with a bedroom and a whole lot to do with a bridegroom. For almost as long as I've wanted to be an attorney, I have wanted to be a wife. When I was younger, I often doodled my first and middle name with the last name of the boy that I liked at the time. When I finally got a boyfriend, I wanted him to marry me. In retrospect, we are both glad we didn't make that mistake, but I was still obsessed with marriage. They say that love is blind, but if love is blind, then LUST is a blind, mentally-challenged, deaf mute. Lust doesn't see the obvious. Lust doesn't listen to reason. Lust doesn't say the expected. Lust doesn't think rationally. Lust is all about feelings--and false feelings at that.

Anything can be the subject of lust, and for me, it was marriage. It was flowers and a long white dress. It was someone to spend the rest of my life with. I had an unhealthy obsession with an institution. That obsession melted down my guard and made me flat out stupid, leading to the biggest mistake thus far in my life...my failed marriage. Obviously, more than my insane desire to get married ruined my marriage, but without that lust, I never would have gotten married at that time in my life to that person. I have learned that lust in any form is wrong, even when you are lusting after something that society considers to be a good thing. I mean really, who can argue that wanting to be married is bad? I can.

Wanting to be married to complete your identity is bad. Wanting to be married so much that it clouds your judgment is bad. But most importantly, wanting to be married so bad that you put getting married before your relationship with God can be devastating. I've said it before, and I'll say it again, "God is a jealous God."[38] Though He doesn't want us to be alone, He doesn't want us to put anything (marriage) or anyone (the hunter) before him.

I am stress this because women have been so indoctrinated with the ideas that we need to get married and that a single woman is a second-class citizen that we may not realize that being a married woman is way too high on our priority list. As a result, we may make compromises during our hunt that we wouldn't normally make, all for the sake of not being alone. We may make changes to who we are and who God made us because we are trying to please a man and not God. We may let a hunter pursue us who does not live up to our ideals. We may lose our focus on God because we are focusing on the altar.

I cannot stress enough that if you follow God's will, He will bless you. Convert your passion for being a married woman into a passion for a stronger relationship with Christ, and you cannot go wrong. In a Godly life, there is no lust, and God alone is sufficient.

1. Where does your desire for marriage come from?

2. What is your image of marriage based upon?

3. Acknowledge that there is nothing wrong with a desire for marriage as long as it does not end with the desire for a wedding.

Part Four

CONCLUSION FOR NOW

For me, everything contained herein is a work in progress on a daily basis. I am not perfect, but try to be obedient. I feel that even writing this was an act of obedience. It won't be easy to share my personal trials and weaknesses. It also won't be easy for some people to read this. I promise you that everything I advise applies to me, as much as anyone else.

I would never intentionally stab someone with my words, but, as my father says, "If someone feels stabbed by what you say, then they are standing too close to the knife." If you feel the slightest bit of conviction or familiarity reading this, it is because that which God needed to tell me and I needed to learn is that which God needs you to know as well. I believe that God won't let you go through strife, pain or struggles for no reason, even if you brought the trials on yourself. This book is my testimony, and this my final prayer.

My Prayer

Dear Lord, on the day I sat down to write this, I knew that it would be a blessing to me. You have allowed me to look back long enough to see my mistakes, and to look forward to practicing the lessons You have taught me. Lord, everything I needed to know was right there in Your Word, but at times, I ignored what You had to say because it seemed difficult. Little did I know that when I ignored You, I moved farther away from You, and that's when life really became difficult. I want this writing to bless You and to show Your awesome, merciful, graceful nature. I want other single women to learn that if they will just talk to You, everything will be alright in Your time. Let me continue to see and let them see the blessing of being single and the opportunity to grow closer to You and to love ourselves more. Give us all wisdom about the potential hunters in our lives and about Your ability to provide exactly what we ask for and exactly what we need. Help us to not lose our focus when we are blessed with a relationship, so that we do not fall into the traps of the flesh and this world. Thank You, God for making me go on this journey. Thank You for choosing me. And Thank You for the blessings that the words You have given me will be to other people. In Your Son Jesus' name I pray. *Amen.*

APPENDIX A

STEPS TO COMMITMENT TO CHRIST...SIMPLE AS ABC

Admit that you are separated from God by sin, and the penalty for unforgiven sin is death.

(Read Romans 3:23, 6:23)

Believe that Jesus Christ died on the cross to bridge the gap between God and sinful man.

(Read John 3:16, Romans 5:8, 1 Timothy 2:5,
1 Peter 3:18)

Confess that Jesus Christ is your Lord and Savior.

(Read John 1:12, Romans 10:9, Revelation 3:20)

APPENDIX B - SCRIPTURE REFERENCES

INTRODUCTION
Know Who's In Control of the Forest
1. Proverbs 18:22
2. Ecclesiastes 3:11, 3:8

PART ONE
The Virtuous Woman
3. Proverbs 31:10-31
4. Proverbs 31:10
5. Psalms 103.12
6. Proverbs 31:11
7. Proverbs 31:13-17
8. Proverbs 31:18
9. 1 John 5:2-3
10. Proverbs 31:20, 25-26
11. Proverbs 31:30

A Call to Holiness
12. Luke 1:75
13. 2 Corinthians 7:1
14. Genesis 2:18
15. Psalms 25:14
16. Proverbs 14:26-27
17. Exodus 20:3-5
18. 1 Thessalonians 3:12-13
19. 1 John 4:7-8
20. 1 Corinthians 7:32-34

A Man's Gift Makes Room For Him
1. Proverbs 18:16

Thou Shalt Not Covet
22. Exodus 20:17
23. Galatians 5:17
24. Psalms 37:7-11
25. Philippians 4:13

Enjoy Your "Me Time"
26. Genesis 2:18
27. 1 Thessalonians 5:17

PART TWO
The Ideal Hunter
28. Mark 11:24
29. 1 Samuel 8:7, 22, 1 Samuel 9, 1 Samuel 15

A Piece of Coal vs. A Slug
30. Psalm 37:4-5.

Small Group
Study Guide

A Six-Week Study of
Pray While You're Prey
by
Toni L. Wortherly, Esquire

***Participants should have the book and study guide
prior to the first discussion***

© 2012 Toni L. Wortherly

Pray While You're Prey Study Guide

Week One

Name: _____

What do you expect or hope to learn, gain, or take away from this course?

_____
_____
_____
_____
_____
_____
_____
_____
_____
_____
_____
_____

It's the beginning of a new year. Name five things you want to let go of from your past, and what you will replace them with this year.

Letting Go	Replacing With

Knowing Who's In Control of the Forest:
Read: Proverbs 18:22, Ecclesiastes 3, and
Jeremiah 29:11 As you read, make note of any
Scripture that particularly impacts you. Then
answer the following questions:

1. Do you believe in Jesus Christ--that He died
    for your sins and is the living Son of God? If
    your answer is 'Yes,' move on to question 2.
    If your answer is no, turn to Appendix A to
    find out more about committing your life to
    Christ, and please speak to a facilitator,
    deacon, or minister, if you have the desire to
    make that commitment. Without a
    commitment to Christ, it is difficult, if not
    impossible, for this book and study to be
    effective.

2. Do you believe that God is sovereign and
    that He has a plan for your life?

3. Name instances in which God showed you
    that He is in control.
    Specific Instances Where God showed He is
in Control
    1.
    2.
    3.
    4.
    5.

Why this Class? Why Now?
1. Now that you know why I wrote this
    book, take a few minutes to focus on
    your reasons for reading this book.
2. Do you know what has influenced your
    relationship expectations?
3. What is the biggest mistake you have ever
    made? Say it out loud if you feel
    comfortable (write it down if you do not).
    Forgive yourself out loud. Pray to God
    for His forgiveness and believe that He
    has forgiven you. Move on.

Pray While You're Prey Study Guide
Week Two

Name: _____

A Virtuous Woman (and a Godly Man)
Women: Read Proverbs 31 in its entirety. Men:
Read 1 Timothy 3:8-13. As you read, make note
of any Scripture that particularly impacts you.

1. List the characteristics in the passage. Which
    of these attributes do you possess?

2. Ask God to reveal the areas that you need to
    improve upon and bless you in your efforts.

What I Possess	What Needs Work

3. What, besides your sin, are you beating yourself up about?

List ten things that are wonderful about you. Focus on these things, and others will too.
1.
2.
3.
4.
5.
6.
7.
8.
9.
10.

A Call to Holiness
Read: Luke 1:75, 2 Corinthians 7:1, Genesis 2:18, Psalms 25:14, Proverbs 14:26-27, Exodus 20:3-5, 1 Thessalonians 3:12-13, 1 John 4:7-8, 1 Corinthians 7:32-34. As you read, make note of any Scripture that particularly impacts you.

1. Take an inventory of your spiritual life.
   a) Do you pray regularly?
   b) Do you attend church regularly?
   c) Do you give of your time, talent and tithe regularly?

2. What area(s) of your spiritual life could use some help? What can you do to improve those areas?

What Needs Work	How Can I Improve

3. What are some ministries (not necessarily in the church) in which you feel you would be effective?

Pray While You're Prey Study Guide
Week Three

Name: _____

A Man's Gift Makes Room for Him
Read Proverbs 18:16. As you read, make note of
any Scripture that particularly impacts you.

1. WOMEN: Which characteristic do you
    identify with the most--independent,
    controlling, or needy?
    GUYS: Which characteristic do you find the
    most annoying --independent, controlling, or
    needy?

2. What are the positive aspects of that
characteristic? What are the negative aspects of
that characteristic?

Positive	Negative

3. How has that characteristic affected your past
relationships and your relationship with Christ?

Thou Shalt Not Covet
Read Exodus 20:17; Galatians 5:17; Psalms 37:7-11; Philippians 4:13. As you read, make note of any Scripture that particularly impacts you.

1. What is the difference between happiness and contentment?

2. Have you learned to be content in every situation? If so, please share how.

3. Ask God to help you realize that His children have everything they need.

Enjoy Your "Me Time"
Read Genesis 2:18; 1 Thessalonians 5:17. As you read, make note of any Scripture that particularly impacts you.

1. What are your favorite activities? How much time do you spend doing them?

2. What are your goals for the next five years?

   Ten years?
   Twenty years?
   Are you working toward them?

3. Give yourself at least an hour each day to focus on you. Clear your mind of what has to be done for everyone else, if possible.

Pray While You're Prey Study Guide
Week Four

Name: _____

A Hunting License
1. What are you looking for in your relationships (socializing, camaraderie, marriage)?

2. *If there is someone special in your life, ask God to reveal what he or she is looking for, because sometimes people say what they think you want to hear.*

3. What has been the result in relationships in which you and your mate wanted different things?

The Ideal Hunter
Read Mark 11:24; 1 Samuel 8:7, 22, 1; Samuel 9; 1 Samuel 15. As you read, make note of any Scripture that particularly impacts you.

1. WOMEN: Imagine that you are preparing for a date and he arrives early. Would God, as your father, let your dates in? Do the men you date meet His standards?
2. MEN: Imagine that you are preparing for a date. Would God, as your father, let you go? Do the women you date meet His standards?

3. Describe your ideal mate in every detail you can think of? *Review your list to make sure that saved, sanctified and separated are on that list.*

4. *Pray that God will send the mate you desire, not what others want for you.*

A Piece of Coal vs. A Slug
Read Psalm 37:4-5. As you read, make note of any Scripture that particularly impacts you.

1. Do you attract more coal (diamonds in the rough) or slugs? Why do you think that is?

2. *Ask God for the gift of discernment, so that you can tell the difference.*

Animal Instincts
1. Review the list of predators. Do any of them seem familiar? Which ones? Do you share their characteristics?

2. Which predators do you attract the most? The ones that work for you? The ones that prey on your weaknesses? The ones that give up on a challenge?

3. WOMEN: What hunting methods do you respond to the most? Is that good or bad? MEN: What hunting methods do you use the most? Is that good or bad?

Pray While You're Prey Study Guide
Week Five

Name: _____

Open Season
Read Song of Solomon 1:2, 7, 10, 16, Song of
Solomon 8:7. As you read, make note of any
Scripture that particularly impacts you.

1. What is the biggest challenge posed by being
single (i.e. loneliness, temptation)? *If you are not
challenged by your singleness, say a prayer of thanksgiving.*

Combating Loneliness
Read John 14:26, Isaiah 41:10. As you read, make
note of any Scripture that particularly impacts
you.

1. What is the difference between being alone
and being lonely?

2. If you are a child of God, are you ever alone?

Anytime you feel lonely or alone, ask God to comfort you.

Focus Focus Focus
Read Exodus 20:5, Matthew 14:29-31. As you
read, make note of any Scripture that particularly
impacts you.

1. What aspects of your relationships cause you to lose focus on God?
If you are in a relationship, make a pact with your mate that you will keep God first in your relationship.
If you are not in a relationship, focus on weak areas in your relationship with Christ while you are waiting for him to send your hunter.

Being Chaste While Being Chased
Read. 1 Thessalonians 4:3. As you read, make note of any Scripture that particularly impacts you.
Right now, make a commitment to Christ that your will keep you body pure until you are married.
1. If you are extremely sensitive to sexual innuendo, make a list of movies, television shows, magazines, etc. that you need to avoid.

The Lust for Marriage
Read Exodus 20:5. As you read, make note of any Scripture that particularly impacts you.
1. Where does your desire for marriage come from?

2. What is your image of marriage based upon?

Acknowledge that there is nothing wrong with a desire for marriage as long as it does not end with the desire for a wedding.

Pray While You're Prey Study Guide

Week Six

Name: _____

Conclusion for Now
Write a prayer of admiration for who God is to
you.

Write a prayer of confession for the thing which
you seek God's forgiveness.

Write a prayer of thanksgiving for your journey
so far and the journey ahead.

Write a prayer of supplication for what you will need while you are prey (women) or while you are hunting (men).

Feel free to share any of these prayers with your group.

Scriptural References for Weekly Study

Week One - Intro
Know Who's In Control
of the Forest
1. Proverbs 18:22
2. Ecclesiastes 3:11, 3:8
Jeremiah 29:11

Week Two - Prayers for
the Hunted
PART ONE
The Virtuous Woman
3. Proverbs 31:10-31
4. Proverbs 31:10
5. Psalms 103.12
6. Proverbs 31:11
7. Proverbs 31:13-17
8. Proverbs 31:18
9. 1 John 5:2-3
10. Proverbs 31:20, 25-26
11. Proverbs 31:30
1 Timothy 3:8-13

A Call to Holiness
12. Luke 1:75
13. 2 Corinthians 7:1
14. Genesis 2:18
15. Psalms 25:14
16. Proverbs 14:26-27
17. Exodus 20:3-5
18. 1 Thessalonians 3:12-13
19. 1 John 4:7-8
20. 1 Corinthians 7:32-34
Week Three - Prayers
for the Hunted
A Man's Gift Makes
Room For Him

21. Proverbs 18:16

Thou Shalt Not Covet
22. Exodus 20:17
23. Galatians 5:17
24. Psalms 37:7-11
25. Philippians 4:13

Enjoy Your "Me Time"
26. Genesis 2:18
27. 1 Thessalonians 5:17

Week Four - Prayers for
the Hunter
PART TWO
The Ideal Hunter
28. Mark 11:24
29. 1 Samuel 8:7, 22, 1
Samuel 9, 1 Samuel 15

A Piece of Coal vs. A
Slug
30. Psalm 37:4-5.

Week Five - Prayers
during Hunting Season
PART THREE
Open Season
31. Song of Solomon
1:2, 7, 10, 16
32. Song of Solomon 8:7

Combating Loneliness
33. John 14:26
34. Isaiah 41:10

Focus Focus Focus
35. Exodus 20:5
36. Matthew 14:29-31

ABOUT THE AUTHOR

Toni LaShaun Wortherly is a 27-year-old attorney from Jacksonville, Florida. She accepted Christ at age 11, but her real commitment to Christ did not happen until recently. Toni has been writing since she was 16, and she is also an actress, appearing on stage and in commercials. God has been working on her and with her to combine the gifts that He's given her and the skills that law school taught her for the uplifting of His Kingdom.

10th Anniversary Update

Toni Lashaun Wortherly is now an educator, songwriter and praise team leader. She continues to use God's gifts for the building of His Kingdom, encouraging others through songs, devotions and blogs.

www.tonilashaunmusic.com

Made in the USA
Middletown, DE
24 April 2020

91382819R00068